The Way To God's Heart

by
Pastor McNeal

AuthorHouse™
1663 Liberty Drive
Bloomington, IN 47403
www.authorhouse.com
Phone: 833-262-8899

Because of the dynamic nature of the Internet, any web addresses or links contained in this book may have changed since publication and may no longer be valid. The views expressed in this work are solely those of the author and do not necessarily reflect the views of the publisher, and the publisher hereby disclaims any responsibility for them.

Any people depicted in stock imagery provided by Getty Images are models, and such images are being used for illustrative purposes only.
Certain stock imagery © Getty Images.

This book is printed on acid-free paper.

ISBN: 978-1-4259-4948-8 (sc)

Print information available on the last page.

Published by AuthorHouse 02/07/2022

authorHOUSE®

The Way to God's heart -   I John 4:12

1. Accept: **Romans 15:7**
2. Pursue things that Build up one another: **Romans 14:19**
3. Be Hospitable to one another without complaint: **I Peter 4:9**
4. Be Bearing with one another: **Colossians: 3:13**
5. Forgive one another: **Colossians: 3:13**
6. Regard one another more important than yourself: **Philippians: 2:3**
7. Greet one another with a holy kiss: **Romans 16:16**
                                                         II Corinthian 3:12
                                                         I Corinthians 16:20
8. Be subject to one another: **Ephesians 5:21**
9. Admonish one another: **Romans 15:14**
10. Give preference to one another: **Romans 12:10**
11. Show forbearance to one another in love: **Ephesians 4:2**
12. Be kind to one another: **Ephesians 4:32**
13. Be of the same mind toward one another: **Romans 12:16, 15:5**
14. Be devoted to one another: **Romans 12:10**
15. Have fellowship with one another: **I John 1:7**
16. Clothe yourselves with humility toward one another: **I Peter :5**
17. Stimulate one another to love and good deeds: **Hebrews 10:24**
18. Bear one another's burdens: **Galatians 6:2**
19. Confess your sins to one another: **James 5:16**
20. Have the same care for one another: **I Corinthians 12:25**
21. Encourage on another day by day: **Hebrews 3:13; 10:25**
                               I Thessalonians 5:11
22. Serve one another: **Galatians 5:13**
                          I Peter 4:10
23. Live in peace with one another: **Mark 9:50**
24. Comfort one another: **I Thessalonians 4:18**
25. Wash one another's feet: **John 13:14**
26. Pray for another: **James 5:15**
27. We are members of one another: **Romans 12:5**
28. Do not envy one another: **Galatians 5:26**
29. Do not challenge one another: **Galatians 5:26**
30. Do not judge one another: **Romans 14:13**
31. Do not complain about one another: **James 5:9**
32. Do not speak against one another: **James 4:11**
33. Do not lie to one another: **Colossians 3:9**
34. Love one another: **John 13:34, 35; 15:12, 17**
               I Thessalonians 3:12, 4:9
               I Peter 1:22
               I John 3:11, 23; 4:7, 11, 12
               II John 1:5

The Way to God's heart - I John 4:12

1. Accept: **Romans 15:7**
   Wherefore receive ye one another as Christ also receive
   us to the glory of God.

2. Pursue things that build up one another: **Romans 14:19**
   Let us therefore follow after the thing which make for
   peace, and things wherewith one may edify another.

3. Be hospitable to one another without complaint: **I Peter 4:9**
    Use hospitality to one another without grudging.

4. Be bearing with one another: **Colossians: 3:13**
    Forbearing one another, and forgiving one another,
    if any man have a quarrel against any; even as Christ
    forgave you, so also do ye.

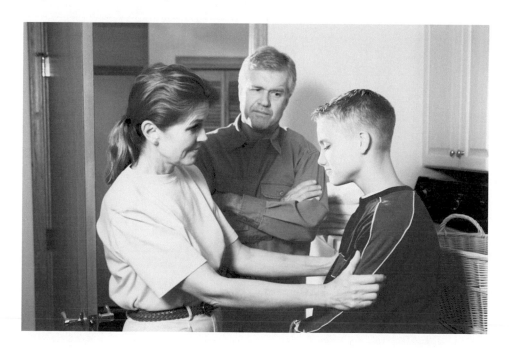

5. Forgive one another: **Colossians: 3:13**
> Forbearing one another, and forgiving one another,
> if any man have a quarrel against any; even as
> Christ forgave you, so also do ye.

6. Regard one another more important than yourself: **Philippians: 2:3**
> Let nothing be done though strife or vainglory;
> but in lowliness of mind let each esteem other
> better than themselves.

7. Greet one another with a holy kiss: **Romans 16:16**
II Corinthian 3:12
I Corinthians 16:20

Romans: 16:16   Salute one another with an holy kiss. The churches of Christ salute you.

II Corinthian: 3:12   Seeing then that we have such hope, we use great plainness of speech.

I Corinthian: 16:20   All the brethren greet you. Greet ye one another with a holy kiss.

8. Be subject to one another. **Ephesians 5:21**
Submitting yourselves one to another in the fear of God

9.   Admonish one another. **Romans 15:14**
     And I myself also am persuaded of you. My brethren,
     that ye also are full of goodness, filled with all knowledge,
     able also to admonish one another.

10. Give preference to one another: **Romans 12:10**
     Be kindly affectioned one to another with brotherly
     love; in honor preferring one another;

11. Show forbearance to one another in love: **Ephesians 4:2**
> With all lowliness and meekness; with longsuffering,
> forbearing one another in love

12. Be kind to one another: **Ephesians 4:32**
> And be ye kind one to another tenderhearted,
> forgiving one another, even as God for Christ's
> sake hath forgiven you.

13. Be of the same mind toward one another: **Romans 12:16, 15:5**

> **Romans 12:16** Be of the same mind one toward another. Mind not high things, but condescend to men of low estate. Be not wise in your own conceits.

> **Romans 15:15** Nevertheless, brethren, I have written the more boldly unto you in some sort, as putting you in mind, because of the grace that is give to me of God.

14. Be devoted to one another: **Romans 12:10**
> Be kindly affectioned one to another with brotherly love; in honour preferring one another;

15. Have fellowship with one another: **I John 1:7**
    But if walk in the light, as he is in the light, we have fellowship one with another, and the blood of Jesus Christ his son cleanses us from all sin.

16. Clothe yourselves with humility toward one another: **I Peter 5:5**
    Likewise, ye younger, submit yourselves unto the elder. Yea, all of you be subject one to another, and be clothed with humility: for God resisteth the proud, and giveth grace to the humble.

17. Stimulate one another to love and good deeds: **Hebrews 10:24**
      And let us consider one another to provoke
      unto love and to good works.

18. Bear one another's burdens: **Galatians 6:2**
      Bear ye one another's burdens and so fulfill
      the law of Christ.

19. Confess your sins to one another: **James 5:16**
        Confess your faults one to another, and pray one for
        another, that ye may be healed. The effectual fervent
        prayer of a righteous man availeth much.

20. Have the same care for one another: **I Corinthians 12:25**
        That there should be no schism in the body;
        but that the members should have the same
        care one for another.

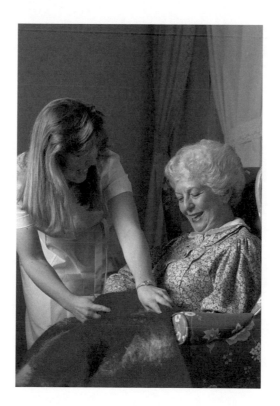

21. Encourage one another day by day:
Hebrews 3:13; 10:25
I Thessalonians 5:11

Hebrews 3:13 But exhort one another daily while it is called to day; lest any of you be hardened through the deceitfulness of sin.

Hebrews 10:25 Not forsaking the assembling of ourselves together, as the manner of some is; but exhorting one another; and so much the more, as ye see the day approaching.

I Thessalonians 5:11 Wherefore comfort yourselves together, and edify one another, even as also ye do.

22. Serve one another: **Galatians 5:13**
                     I Peter 4:10

   Galatians 5:13 for, brethren, ye have been called unto
                     liberty; only use not liberty for an occasion to the
                     flesh, but by love serve one another.

   I Peter 4:10   As every man hath received the gift,
                     even so minister the same one to another, as good
                     steward of the manifed grace of God.

23. Live in peace with one another: **Mark 9:50**
             Salt is good: but if the salt have lost his saltness,
             wherewith will ye season it? Have salt in yourselves, and
             have peace one with another

24. Comfort one another: **I Thessalonians 4:18**

> Wherefore comfort one another with these words.

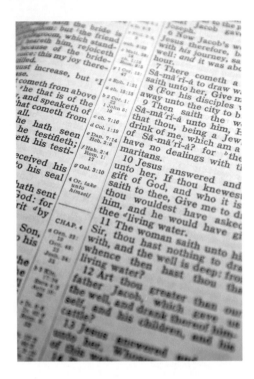

25. Wash one another's feet: **John 13:14**

> If I then, your Lord and Master have washed your
> feet; ye also ought to wash one another's feet.

26. Pray for another: **James 5:16**

> Confess your faults one to another and pray one for
> another, that ye may be healed. The effectual fervent
> prayer of a righteous man availeth much.

27. We are members of one another: **Romans 12:5**

> So we, being many, are one body in Christ, and every
> one members one of another.

28. Do not envy one another: **Galatians 5:26**
        Let us not be desirous of vain glory, provoking one
        another, envying one another.

29. Do not challenge one another: **Galatians 5:26**
        Let us not be desirous of vain glory provoking one
        another envying one another.

30. Do not judge one another: **Romans 14:13**
> Let us no therefore judge one another any more;
> but judge this rather, that no man put a stumbling
> block or an occasion to fall in his brother's way.

31. Do not complain about one another: **James 5:9**
> Grudge not one against another, brethren,
> lest ye be condemned: behold, the judge
> standeth before the door.

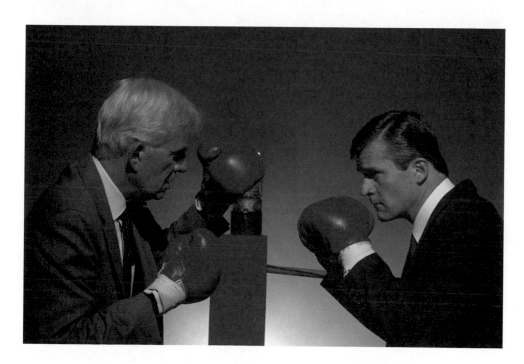

32. Do not speak against one another **James 4:11**
> Speak not evil one of another, brethren. He that
> speaketh evil of his brother, and judgeth his brother, speak evil of the
> law: but if thou judge the law, thou are not a doer of
> the law, but a judge.

33. Do not lie to one another: **Colossians 3:9**
> Lie not one to another, seeing that ye have put
> off the old man with his deeds.

34. Love one another: **John 13:34, 35; 15:12, 17**
                            Romans 13:8
                            I Thessalonians 3:12, 4:9
                            I Peter 1:22
                            I John 3:11, 23
                            I John 4:7, 11, 12
                            II John 1:5

John 13:34   A new commandment I give unto you,
                 that ye love one another; as I have loved you,
                 that ye also love one another.

John 13:35   By this shall all men know that ye are my
                 disciples, if ye have love one to another.

John 15:12   This is my commandment, That ye love
                 one another, as I have loved you.

John 15:17   These thing I command you, that ye love one another.

Romans 13:8   Owe no man any thing, but to love one another:
                  For he that loveth another hath fulfilled the law.

I Thessalonians 3:12 And the Lord make you to increase and abound in
                          love one toward another, and toward all men, even as
                          we do toward you;

I Thessalonians 4:9 But as touching brotherly love ye need not that I
                         write unto you: For ye yourselves are taught of
                         God to love one another.

I Peter 1:22   Seeing ye have purified your soul in obeying
                   the truth through the spirit unto unfeigned love
                   of the brethren, see that ye love one another with a
                   pure heart fervently.

I John 3:11   For this is the message that ye heard from the
                  beginning, that we should love one another.

I John 3:23   And this is his commandment that we should belive on
                  the name of his son Jesus Christ, and love one another,
                  as he gave us commandment.

I John 4:7   Beloved, let us love one another: for love is
                 of God; and every one that loveth is born of
                 God, and knoweth God.

I John 4:11   Beloved, if God so loved us, we ought also to love one another.

I John 4:12   No man hath seen God at any time
                    If we love one another, God dwelleth in us,
                    and his love is perfected in us.

II John 1:5   And now I beseech thee, lady, not as though
                    I wrote a new commandment unto thee, but that
                    which we had from the beginning, that we
                    love one another.

Printed in the United States
by Baker & Taylor Publisher Services